BEN WICKS' BOOK OF LOSERS

BEN WICKS' BOOK OF LOSERS

by Ben Wicks

McCLELLAND AND STEWART

All rights reserved
McClelland and Stewart Limited
The Canadian Publishers
25 Hollinger Road
Toronto, Ontario
M4B 3G2

CANADIAN CATALOGUING IN PUBLICATION DATA

Wicks, Ben, 1926-
  Ben Wicks' book of losers

ISBN 0-7710-8993-7

1. Canadian wit and humor, Pictorial.   I. Title.

NC1449.W53A4 1979   741.5'971   C79-094615-7

Printed and bound in the United States of America

Contents

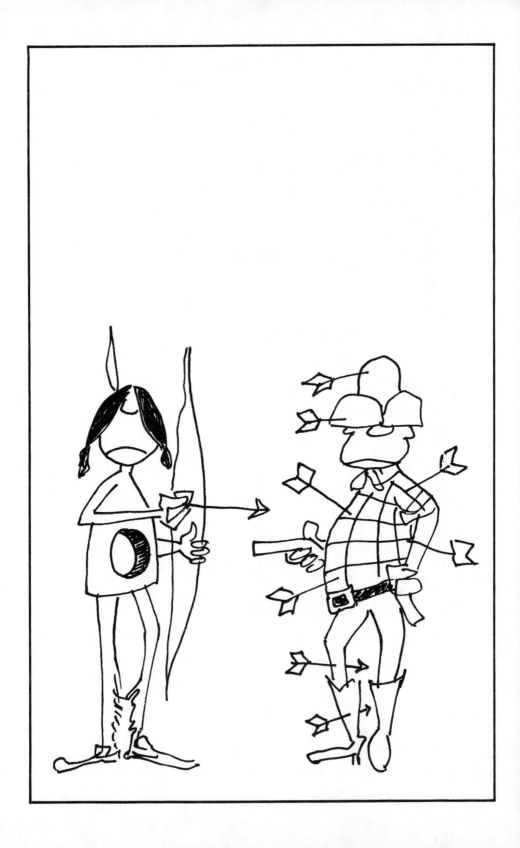

Losers come in all sizes. Small, short, dark, fair, ugly, and pretty. No one and nothing is immune to the tag of "loser."

We live in a world of losers constantly striving to attain the position of winner, completely unaware that to be in front does not guarantee an automatic lift to the winners' plateau.

Let's begin with the obvious. Sport.

To end the race in the first place is to push the body to its maximum effort in order to arrive at the finishing line first. First of what? First of a group it was necessary to pass in order to finish first. Without this group of losers there are no winners.

And what of battle? To win a battle without the help of the defeated is impossible. The mistakes of the losing generals give the winners the opportunity to win the battle.

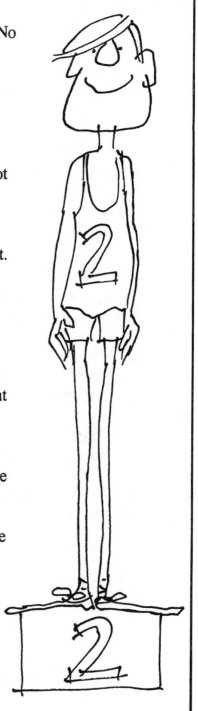

Without the help of the loser no battle is ever won.
From every side we, the losers, are bombarded with news
of the latest exploits and achievements of winners, yet
behind this facade of victory
lie the bodies of unheralded losers.
Nowhere have these unsung heroes
of the world of losers been recognized.
It is my sincere wish that this
book will help to rectify this failing.
In preparing this book I have attempted
to show that, as losers, we are not
alone.

If you have lost a leg – so did
America's greatest actress, Sarah
Bernhardt.

If you have lost an eye, so did
Britain's greatest admiral.

If you have lost your figure, you
should know that Mae West needed five-inch
shoes to lift up her 5 foot 3 inch height
and wore a specially-designed corset
to lift her breasts.

Are you worried by a sex problem? Consider the loser
who wrote to a newspaper telling the world that he neither
drank nor smoked and yet did not seem to be able to
overcome the sex impulse. "Is this due to catarrh, and will
a diet of vegetables and salads help abate it?" Remember,
you have still to utter your last words. Unlike Schubert,
you still have time to finish unfinished business.
So, losers of the world unite.
There's always someone worse off than you.

Since the day Adam first clamped his teeth around the core of an apple, those who have followed have felt that love makes the world go round. It is true that the world is turning, but anyone taking a close look will find that the ride itself is far from smooth. The fact is, love is not as enduring as the poets would have us believe. Like the humps of a camel, love has its ups and downs.

A bliss that finds a lover and his lass romping in the hay sizzles and begins to burn itself out with the passing years. Eyes that were once the colour of rose petals begin to look like bicycle pedals.

A nose that was once the shape of Robert Redford's becomes so repulsive that nothing short of removal seems to be the answer ...

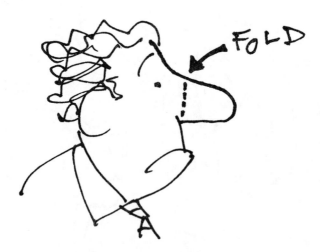

Antonio Laina of Naples, Italy, awoke one morning to find his wife removing his nose with a pair of scissors. "She was jealous," explained Antonio to the hospital surgeons who stitched his nose back onto his face.

Am I unreasonable? I have been married for twelve years and have a family, and my husband recently asked me to be intimate with him on the back seat of our car. This happened in the heart of the country and I agreed. I am now worried because I am sure this is very wrong. Please help me.
(Letter to the *Daily Mirror*, London, England.)

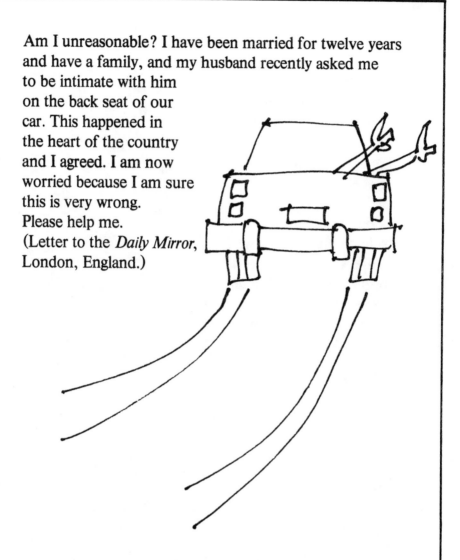

Thinking that a good scare might excite her husband more effectively toward sex, a woman in Hamburg, West Germany, hid in the bedroom and greeted her husband with a blood curdling shriek as he walked in after work. The startled husband bolted, tripped over a chair, and fell through the window. He was in the hospital for a week.

Just Filmz Inc. is a verbal massage parlour in downtown Chicago. If you're a male, $15 buys you twenty minutes of non-stop dirty talk from the hostess of your choice. For an additional $5 she will do the talking topless. Jason Irwin, the owner of Just Filmz says most of the women who work for him are ex-telephone operators. "They're naturals," he claims.

Police in Marseille, France, raided a brothel for the elderly. Two prostitutes in their late fifties and eight customers ranging from sixty to seventy-seven-year-olds were jailed.

The twenty-eight-year-old brother of the Duke Of Argyl, Lord Colin Cambell, left his bride of nine months after a whirlwind New York courtship. "I proposed to her across a candle-lit table in a restaurant at 3 o'clock in the morning and with twelve pints of draft Guinness under my belt," Lord Colin told *The People*, a mass circulation London newspaper. "We spent our first night together as man and wife at a hotel in Philadelphia. She became the most passionate wife I could possibly hope that she might be, but alas. Our fairy-tale marriage began to disintegrate when twenty-five-year-old Georgie, my wife, confessed that she had been a boy until the age of eighteen and had undergone a sex change. The only thing now," said the Lord, "is to pick up the pieces. I have to be married to a woman who can give me a family. This is a responsibility to the Argyl Clan."

At the Chester Assizes in England a girl was asked by the judge why she took off her petticoat in her boy-friend's car on a Saturday night. She replied, "It was rather an expensive one and I knew what we were going to do. I asked him to take it off as I didn't want it to get crumbled." In reporting this the *London Observer* went on to say that "this behaviour can be ascribed to artificial development. Outside questionable growth. Boosters on cows that produce far more milk than they were designed to do. Battery hens that never see the light of day and now overdeveloped children almost stuffed with vitamins from birth. With our own suitable climate they were never intended to reach sexual maturity until at least fifteen."

Wanted. Playpen cot and chair. Also two separate beds. (*Evening Standard*)

The wife told the judge that after confessing to her husband about her adultery with an itinerant ice-cream seller, she wrote a letter to the ice-cream man ending the association. She gave it to her husband, who took it to the man, shook hands with him, and came back with two six-penny cornets. (*Evening News*)

Dr. David S. Love, assistant professor of anatomy at Case Western Reserve University School of Medicine, was indicted for involuntary manslaughter in the death of his wife. He had suspended his wife Virginia, who was nude, from a third-floor window of their home in Cleveland Heights by a rope tied around her ankle, in order to perform a sex act. The rope slipped from Love's hand and Mrs. Love fell to her death. The cause of her death was a torn liver, according to the coroner. Love was charged with involuntary manslaughter after the newspaper boy on his street reported that he had seen the Loves perform the act twice before. Dr. Love's lawyer, Elmer A. Guiliani, said, "Whatever happened certainly doesn't indicate that Dr. Love is guilty of anything." (*Cleveland Plain Dealer*)

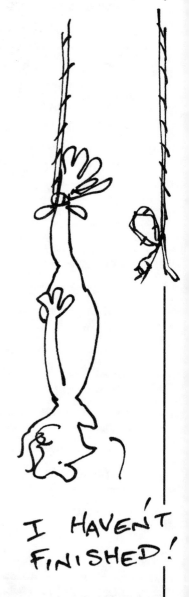

I HAVEN'T FINISHED!

Demetrius Soupolos, a Greek guest worker in Stuttgart, and his wife, Traute, wanted a child badly. After a long period of trying without success, Soupolos consulted a physician, who pronounced the young Greek sterile. Soupolos then convinced his wife, Traute, and his neighbour, Frank Maus, that the latter should accept $2,500 to mate with the former so that she might become pregnant. Maus, who was married and had two children, copulated with Traute faithfully three evenings a week for six months. Nothing came of it. Soupolos insisted Maus submit to a medical examination, whereupon it was discovered Maus was also sterile. It was then that any luck that the generous Maus may have had began to vanish. First he lost the company of his neighbour's wife, Traute. His wife was forced to confess that their two children had been fathered by another man, and as if this were not enough, Soupolos sued him for breach of contract. (*Parade*)

Frank Speck, of Philadelphia, Pa. had a vasectomy operation in April, 1974. His doctor assured him that he and his wife would no longer need to use contraceptive methods. Mrs. Speck became pregnant several months later. Mrs. Speck decided to have an abortion, which was performed in December by a second doctor. Shortly thereafter she gave birth to a daughter, Francine.
The Specks are suing both physicians.
(*Philadelphia Evening Bulletin*)

A near-naked man and his woman companion were trapped in a tiny sports car when the man was suddenly immobilized by a slipped disc, pinning his lover beneath him. The desperate woman tried to summon help by honking the horn with her foot. A doctor, ambulance man, fireman, and a group of passers-by quickly surrounded the couple's car. After being helped out of the car and into a coat, the distraught woman sobbed, "How am I going to explain to my husband what has happened to his car?" (*Toronto Globe and Mail*)

Mary Jane Williams offered police an unusual excuse when they finally stopped her after a lengthy chase at speeds up to seventy miles an hour. She told them that she had assumed the wailing sound of the sirens was the screaming of her boyfriend, who had been clinging to the luggage rack of her car since she had driven off during an argument. (*UPI*)

Police have arrested eighteen-year-old Mrs. Phakar Khemawong on a charge of cutting off her husband's penis while he was asleep at their home in Bangkae, Thailand. The incident reportedly followed a heated argument over Mr. Phakar's alleged extramarital activities. She waited until the early hours of the morning, when she allegedly cut off her husband Aroon's penis with a kitchen knife and threw it out of the bedroom window. A neighbour heard Aroon's screams of pain and rushed him to a local hospital. There, a doctor advised the neighbour to go back and fetch the severed organ. The neighbour hurried back and was just in time to retrieve the penis from the beak of a duck. Police detained Mrs. Phakar for further questioning. (*Bangkok Post*)

An English court granted a divorce to Doris and Albert May, who'd been married for twenty-six years, after Doris charged that Albert ran around naked playing the tambourine outside their house whenever she rejected his sexual advances, and Albert charged that Doris made him pay £4 each time that they slept together. Irreconcilable differences, ruled the judge. (*Memphis Commercial Appeal*)

Hu, wife of a Taiwanese man named Wu, left home after a heated quarrel with her husband. Wu went to the nearby city of Kaohsiung in search of his wife. Failing to find her, he checked into a hotel and asked that a call girl be sent to his room. The call girl turned out to be Hu, and after a second heated argument, Hu and Wu returned home together "for fear of losing face." (*China Post*)

Seven hundred love letters written by a young Taiwanese man to his girlfriend have finally brought results. The girl has become engaged to the postman who delivered the letters. (*San Francisco Chronicle*)

A young Yugoslavian named Dorsun Yilmaz recently made arrangements to elope with his beloved, the daughter of one of his neighbours in the town of Dalmali. Sometime after midnight, a shadowy figure wrapped in a blanket descended the ladder he had placed by her window; he carried her to his waiting car, and they sped away. Several miles down the road he unwrapped the delectable bundle and discovered that he was carrying off the girl's grandmother, who beat him up. (*The Sun*)

One of the greatest problems for a
loser is knowing when he has finally rid himself of
the label. Just when he thinks he's made it
into the winner's circle an unknown arm will
slip around his back and take the prize.

Women Have More To Lose Than Men

A twenty-five-year-old woman told a Supreme Court of Ontario all-male jury how two men had held her captive in a Toronto hair-dressing salon. After being forced to commit indecent acts with both men the woman was taken to the back room by the hairdresser who then yanked off her clothes and raped her. After that, she said, the hairdresser totalled her bill  for a hair-set. Five dollars. She was asked if she paid the bill before leaving the shop. "Of course I paid it," she replied.

A seventy-one-year-old woman in Miami was so angry with a youth who blew smoke in her face on a bus that she whipped out a can of mace and set off after him. Although the youth escaped the woman did manage to spray six fellow passengers with a full-face dose of the gas, sending them to hospital.

An English magistrate said, dismissing a charge of assault brought by a woman against her husband, "It is not unreasonable, in a certain class, for a woman to have her face smacked from time to time, and to be punched about. It is the normal wear and tear of their married life."

The defendant was said to have been seen leaving a butcher shop with six chickens in his basket. He had not paid for them. On being asked why he was stealing six chickens he answered, "I had a row with the wife and was taking the chickens home to throw at her."

Sixty women were victims of a bandit in Seattle. After stopping them on the street the villain would remove a single shoe and run off with it into the night. More than sixty single shoes were later found in the apartment of a suspect.

A twenty-five-year-old man broke into the Bronx, New York apartment of a young mother, raped her, and fell asleep on the bed. Police were summoned and woke the snoring intruder with a bucket of ice water. The judge listening to the trial also fell asleep. A mistrial was declared.

I am engaged to a wonderful man, but lately
he has been very moody and is always hitting
me. He says it is nothing to what I shall get
after marriage, and I must get used to being
kept under control.
Please advise me: I want
to marry him, but don't
know how to handle
the situation.
(*Womans Own*)

I am twenty-nine,
single; I neither
drink nor smoke.
I do not seem to
be able to overcome
the sex impulse.
Is this due to
catarrh, and will a
diet of vegetables and salads
help to abate it?
(*Health For All*)

A seventeen-year-old bride married four months before
she discovered her nineteen-year-old "husband" was a
woman has been granted an annulment. Chancellor D. J.
Alissandratos ordered the marriage annulled – based on
a Tennessee law forbidding homosexual marriages –
after reviewing a birth certificate of the young woman's
spouse, showing the husband was born female. The
husband who refused to undress in front of his/her wife

with the lights on, claiming he had a deformity caused by a football injury, was taking male hormones. The young woman, who now works for a Memphis restaurant, was asked during the hearing only if she knew her spouse was a woman when they married in 1978. "No, ma'am," she told lawyer Audrey Scott. The minister who married the couple said the discovery the bridegroom was a woman came as a complete shock to him, the bride, and his congregation. (*UPI*)

A man who testified three years ago in a divorce case in Montpellier, France, that he had slept with a woman whose husband had accused her of adultery was recently found guilty of perjury. The man, André Loisel, had stated under oath that he had had sexual relations with the woman in a Paris hotel. The woman denied the charge. At Loisel's trial for perjury, he was asked to describe the incident. He did so, but he neglected to mention the fact that the woman had an artificial belly button as the result of an operation several years earlier. The judges ruled that "even in a room where the lights were low this detail could not have gone unnoticed." Loisel received a suspended sentence of three months in jail and a $200 fine. (*New York Post*)

DID YOU LOSE A BUTTON?

Janet Dyson was fined $150 Tuesday and told not to snoop again for a year. Police caught her peering through the mail slot in a neighbour's front door – after her neighbours went to court  to keep her from peeping through their windows. Said Mrs. Margaret Swift, who lives nearby, "She even peers into the garbage can." Mrs. Dyson claims she can't help it – says, "I'll do it again when I feel like it." And, explaining about that letter slot; "I saw the postman delivering letters and I just wanted to look at them and see where they came from." (*UPI*)

In 1956, a Parisian night watchman named Noel Carriou became enraged when his wife cooked a roast too rare and threw her out of bed in the middle of the night. Mme Carriou suffered a broken neck and died. He was sentenced to twelve years at hard labour. Released after seven years because of good behaviour, he remarried. Unfortunately his second wife, Clemence, shared his first wife's fatal lack of cooking skill. After being served a burnt roast, M. Carriou exclaimed, "You cook like a Nazi," and stabbed her to death. M. Carriou has been sentenced to another eight years in prison. (*San Francisco Chronicle*)

The women of Sipche, a village in Northern Nepal, believed that the one-hundredth man they killed would turn into gold and make them rich, and at the same time help them get into heaven. The women apparently lured the men to a feast, at which they were fed dishes mixed with harital, a poisonous root. The village is now entirely inhabited by children and widows. (*London Express*)

Women in Ugley, England, have changed the name of their community organization from Ugley Women's Institute to the Women's Institute (Ugley Division). (*Edmonton Sun*)

A fifty-nine-year-old Sydney, Australia, housewife died of a heart attack in front of the television cameras after learning that she had won the first round of an Australian quiz show called "Temptation." An executive of the TV station said the show, which was being taped at a local studio before a live audience, would not be aired but that "when the relatives recover from the shock, we may offer them the film of the program. I'm sure they would like to see how happy she was." (*San Francisco Chronicle*)

Forty-seven-year-old Elisetto Piuma of Savona, Italy, died from a heart attack brought on by laughing too heartily at a joke-telling contest there. The contest-winning joke was not reported. (*Reuters*)

My husband does not give me
my housekeeping allowance. He
hides it. He puts pound notes
in odd places all over
the house and makes me
look for them. I can
never be quite sure
how many to expect, and
I am scared stiff that
I will miss one or two.
(*Daily Herald*)

For some unfathomable reason most people who can swim, run, jump, kick, or punch are envied by those of us who are content just to be able to crawl from the sack on Monday morning that follows "the night before."

Most of us live for the moment when we are lifted onto a stretcher. Still others watch fascinated as a wet towel is wedged up the snout of a boxer in the forlorn hope that the bleeding will stop long enough to allow the nose to be punched again ... and again ... and again.

Let's shovel aside the sports heroes and look at some facts. All sport is not the be all and end all of what it takes to be a hero. The fact is that most winners in sport have taken advantage of another's misfortune.

Like this report of a golf tournament in England: "The end came at the fourth where Walsh cut his second shot into the famous Pow Burn. Dunlop would have shared the same fate, but by great good fortune, his shot struck a spectator and rebounded onto the green." (*Daily Telegraph*)

A lady golfer competing in the 1912 Shawnee Invitational for Ladies at Shawnee-on-Delaware took a glorious wack at the ball and watched as it sailed majestically into the Binniekill river. But luck was on her side. The ball remained floating, making it possible for the energetic golfer to leap into a boat and set off in hot pursuit. Each time she was within range of the ball our heroine would give an almighty swipe. She eventually connected and sent the ball up onto a small beach, 1½ miles from where she had started. After leaping out of the boat she began to tackle the next hurdle – a forest lying between her ball and the hole. She finally made it in a magnificent 166 strokes for the 130-yard, par 3, 16th hole.

During a wrestling match in Providence, Rhode Island, Stanley Pinto was working himself into a winning position when he accidentally entangled himself in the ropes of the ring. In attempting to struggle free he pinned his own shoulders to the mat for the required three seconds unaided by his opponent who was then declared the winner.

Messieurs Lenfant and Mellant were having a game of
billiards in 1834 when
a terrible argument
broke out.
Both men insisted
that the only way
to settle the quarrel
was by a duel. After
drawing lots to see who
should fire first,
Mellant grabbed a red
billiard ball and took the first throw. It hit poor
Lenfant squarely between the eyes and killed him instantly.

Peter O'Toole, an ex-prize fighter
of Chester, England, finished off
an argument with his friend John
Odee by biting off his nose.

In Lakewood, California, a
man jogged into the office of
the Public Finance Company,
pulled out a gun, and demanded
money from the employees.
He took $800 in cash and left
the office, still
jogging. (*Toronto Star*)

Bird watching has been classed as a "hazardous hobby"
by a British Medical Journal, *The Practitioner.* The
magazine reported the case of a bird watcher so oblivious
to other forms of wildlife that he was eaten by a crocodile.
(*Omaha World-Herald*)

When Evelyn Sullivan, fifty-four, of Sault Ste. Marie, Michigan, blew her nose Saturday night, a .22 caliber bullet came out. Mrs. Sullivan had been standing outside her cabin earlier, when she heard gunfire from some hunters in the distance. Police theorized that a stray bullet ricocheted off several objects and came to rest in Mrs. Sullivan's right nostril. "It must have hit her lip and bounced up into her nose," said State Trooper Duane Baley. (*AP*)

During a debate in the Arkansas State Legislature on how to retain capital punishment in the face of recent federal court decisions, Representative Steve Smith of Huntsville submitted a proposed amendment to the Arkansas State Constitution which would substitute drawing and quartering for the electric chair. The amendment provides that "drawing and quartering shall be performed by tractors, one driven by the Governor, one driven by the Commissioner of the Department of Corrections, one by the foreman of the convicting jury, and one by the Arkansas Sheriff's Association."
In the event that a felon manages to survive this process, the amendment further provides that "molten lead be poured into his or her navel," and the body be disembowelled, beheaded, and the head displayed in the capitol rotunda in Little Rock. The amendment also stipulates that the executions be held in public at either the Fayetteville or Little Rock stadiums. Tickets would be sold, but families of the condemned would be given priority for fifty-yard-line seats. (*National Observer*)

Mrs. Horace Peace received slight injuries when her husband shot her with a shotgun. At first Mrs. Peace would not co-operate with the police and she also refused to go to the hospital for treatment. Later Mrs. Peace went to the authorities and explained that her husband was hunting and "thought I was a rabbit so he shot me." No warrants were filed. (*Dispatch*)

A Brazilian was fishing on the banks of the Rio Negro when his line became snagged in a tree. As he tried to free it, a swarm of wild bees flew out of the tree and attacked him. The man escaped by running into the river, where he was eaten by a school of piranha. (*Edmonton Sun*)

During the Central Iowa Conference high-school championship wrestling tournament, South Tama High ninth-grader Jeff Price was matched against Mike Siewert, of Indianola, in the 105-pound weight division. Siewert had suffered from diarrhoea before the match and in the middle of the first round had an accident which, according to the newspaper report, "left both grapplers with soiled uniforms and difficult wrestling conditions." Price lost, five to three. (*Toledo Chronicle*)

A popular sport in Wales has two opponents standing face to face, grasping each other firmly by the shoulders. At the signal they begin kicking each other in the shins, wearing boots that have been reinforced with metal toe plates. The first one to feel that his shins have had enough of this nonsense releases his grip on the other's shoulders and declares himself the loser.

KICK→

The English boxing champion, Jim Mason, and an American challenger, Joe Coburn, danced around each other for three hours and forty-eight minutes without landing a single punch.

DO YOU COME HERE OFTEN?

After Field Marshal Liber Serenge of the Uruguayan Army
called General Juan Ribas, seventy-seven,
of the same force "a socialist,"
they decided to fight a duel.
Meeting at dawn in Montevideo's
Peoples' Peace Park, the two
soldiers fired 137 rounds at each
other from a distance of twenty-five
paces. Neither man was hurt.
Sources close to General Ribas said that
he aimed high on account of his opponent's
advanced age and, in any case, "both
refused to wear their glasses out of dignity." (*Private Eye*)

Despite the incredible advances in the field of science the medical field still holds the record for the number of unfortunates missing from the winner's circle. There is an obvious reason for this. The prostrate position of most medical losers is a constant reminder that they are running a poor second-best to the healthy, golf-playing doctor dressed in virginal white. Perhaps the best illustration of this was given by the Hungarian satirist George Mikes in his classic book *How to Be an Alien*. He explained how a visiting specialist to an English hospital was touring the wards, surrounded by admiring doctors. As he was about to pass a bed, an elderly male patient lifted himself on an elbow and called across the room, "Excuse me doctor. I know it's none of my business, but how am I?"

Harold Fenby of Leeds England began to lose his hearing twenty years ago. A hospital fitted him with a hearing aid. It just didn't work and Fenby resigned himself to being deaf for almost two decades. Last year the hospital found out what the problem was. They had fitted the hearing aid to the wrong ear. (*Toronto Sun*)

George Schwenk of Los Angeles was treated for five days at a local medical centre for an eye infection and then received a bill for $317 – for the delivery of a baby. "Please correct this error," Schwenk wrote plaintively, "or at least send me my baby."

A London physician was once heard to say, "We operated just in time. Another two days and he would have recovered without us."

A husband suffering from flu saw the doctor, who had just visited him, kiss his wife. The defence lawyer explained what happened next. "Under great provocation my client nearly hit him with a milk bottle, but out of respect for the doctor's profession, he refrained and punched his wife instead." (*Toronto Sun*)

A fifty-year-old brick layer suffered a fatal heart attack after laughing uncontrollably for nearly an hour at "The Goodies," a prime-time television comedy show. His wife told reporters that she planned to write to the show's producers to thank them for making her husbands' last minutes so happy.

A Tokyo motorist drove more than a mile after a collision with another car, stopping only when he noticed his right arm missing. Concerned about being caught for drunk driving, Tsutomu Ebara, twenty-two, sped away from the scene of the crash, although his arm had been severed at the elbow. After they took him to the hospital, police charged him with drunk driving anyway. (*Toronto Sun*)

Loughton, England – Alf Hayford, thirty-seven, recently was awarded £3,200 in damages because his motorcycle injuries to his left wrist have affected his sex life. Mr. Hayford testified that he could no longer support himself on his left hand. He also finds gardening difficult. (*CP*)

A forty-two-year-old man from Ponce, Puerto Rico, came to the local hospital complaining of a pain in his shoulder. When doctors examined him, they discovered two inches of coat-hanger wire protruding from his rectum. An X-ray disclosed that he had a soft-drink bottle protruding into the peritoneal cavity of his lower abdomen. The man eventually admitted that he had attempted to give himself an enema with a carbonated beverage and that the bottle somehow became lodged in his rectal area. When he couldn't get it out, he fashioned a hook from a coat hanger and had his wife fish with it for the bottle. An operation to remove the accumulated flotsam was successful. (*Journal of the American Medical Association*)

Walter Alves Pereira, a forty-nine-year-old uneducated barber in Rio de Janeiro, Brazil, has successfully completed fifteen plastic surgery operations on himself, rebuilding his nose and mouth with skin from his chest, using half a razor blade, a pair of tweezers, and an ordinary needle and thread. Pereira was badly disfigured in a fall down a flight of stairs. He was told that plastic surgery could correct his disfigurement, but he couldn't afford it, so he bought a book on the subject at a local medical centre. "I never had any infections because I boiled everything before using it," he explained. "People said I was crazy ... but I did it so that they would stop calling me names and throwing stones at me." (*Toronto Star*)

Dr. Max Feldman put a patient under anesthesia for dental work, whereupon she grabbed a stranglehold on his testicles. The patient then sued and won a $500 verdict because Dr. Feldman broke her finger in an attempt to free himself. (*Wolfe v. Feldman, City Court of New York, 1936*)

A standard joke became a macabre reality in Tehran when a forty-three-year-old farmer died of shock after receiving a hospital bill. Karam Gholampour was hospitalized with a heart ailment. The day of his release, he collapsed and died after being handed a $1,500 bill for his ten-day hospital stay. (*Stars and Stripes*)

Charles Osborne, seventy-nine, of Breckenridge, Minnesota, has had hiccups for fifty-one years. Osborne said his ordeal began in 1922 when he was butchering a hog. The ninety-six doctors whom the unfortunate Mr. Osborne has consulted have all told him that his esophagus has ruptured and formed a small pocket in which food settles. None of them are willing to perform the very delicate operation required to reverse the condition because of the unusually large number of nerves linked to the pocket and Osborne's age. Osborne has tried, without success, all the traditional remedies, including scaring himself with a gun and drinking a glass of water backwards. "A lot of people told me to pray," he said. (*Muscatine Iowa Journal*)

Robert Harmon of Limestone Cove, Texas, was admitted to the local Veterans' Administration Hospital for treatment of a gunshot wound in the foot. When asked to explain the mishap, Harmon told investigating officers that he was in his bathroom when he noticed a spider on his foot. Since no newspapers were handy to swat the insect, Harmon was forced to shoot it off with a sixteen-gauge shotgun. (*Johnson City Press Chronicle*)

Kenneth Thompson, of Phillips, Texas, drove nearly three hundred miles to Springfield, Illinois, with the partly decomposed body of a woman next to him on his car seat. He took the body to the emergency room at St. John's Hospital in Springfield, saying he thought she might need medical attention. Ambulance attendants found the body with her head next to the driver's seat and her feet dangling from the door. Coroner Norman Richter said that the body was in such a state of decomposition that he would not allow relatives to identify it. "I wouldn't put a family through that," he said. According to Richter, the woman sustained broken ribs, internal hemorrhaging, and other internal injuries. Thompson told police that he drove the woman, identified as Mary Grace Rainey, all the way from Phillips, Texas. "She started to look bad around Litchfield," said Thompson. "She must have been alive in St. Louis because I talked to her then," he added. The car was full of foodstuffs, clothes, and household appliances. A cat was also found in the back seat. (*St. Louis Post-Dispatch*)

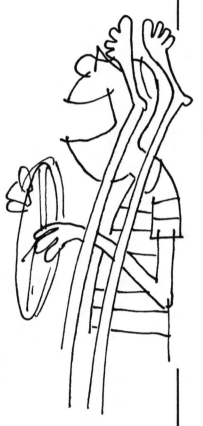

A pathologist who came to examine a corpse ended up a fatality himself in a bizarre incident in Marseille. Shortly before he died of a heart attack, Emile Herve, forty-nine, placed a loaded pistol beside the sink in his kitchen. When the body was discovered, police called Dr. Joseph Cambracedes, sixty-five, for a routine examination. While the doctor stood over Herve's body, an officer opened a window to air out the apartment. The draft caused the kitchen door to slam shut, and the resulting vibrations threw the previously unnoticed pistol to the floor. The gun discharged, and the bullet struck Cambracedes, killing him instantly. (*Sunday Times Advertiser*)

Carmelo Santiago, whose car had stalled on a New York expressway, was beneath his vehicle making repairs when another motorist crashed into it, injuring Carmelo severely. Private ambulance personnel arrived on the scene prior to a city ambulance, and placed him on a stretcher. Shortly thereafter, city personnel insisted the victim be transferred to their stretcher. Private ambulance personnel claimed they were entitled to Carmelo because he was already in their stretcher. City corpsmen, on the other hand, argued that since the private ambulance was overcrowded with members of Carmelo's family, treatment efforts might be hindered en route to the hospital. At the conclusion of a seven-minute discussion, Carmelo was taken aboard the city vehicle, alive. At the conclusion of a trip to the hospital, Carmelo was taken out of the vehicle, dead. (*AP*)

A civil court found Dr. Howard Eddy guilty of medical malpractice and ordered him to pay $175,000 in damages to a patient he had treated for a rectal disorder. Eddy inserted a high-intensity electrical instrument up Richard Schwartz's anal canal when the device came in contact with a pocket of intestinal gas. The gas exploded, blowing out a portion of Schwartz's colon. The court held that Eddy was negligent, in that a reasonable and prudent physician should have foreseen that Schwartz might fart. (*Newsday*)

Sears, Roebuck and Co. has issued warnings to the owners of some 17,000 exercise cycles sold in its stores. According to a spokesman for Sears. " ... after extensive use a metal post under the seat may push through the plastic seat material, exposing the rider to the risk of injury." (*Dallas Morning News*)

Charles Crawley let a passenger out of his car and then backed up, running over the passenger. A passerby shouted at Crawley to stop, but Crawley did not hear the warning because he is deaf. Crawley's passenger did not see the car because he is blind. (*Trentonian*)

A British schoolboy was unable to remove a vase that had become stuck on his head, and was subsequently rushed to the hopsital in a city bus. In order to normalize his appearance in front of other passengers, the boy's mother placed his school cap on top of the vase. (*Edmonton Sun*)

A doctor in Toronto confessed at a coroner's inquest that a collapsed patient's bad breath prevented him from doing close mouth-to-mouth resuscitation. Dr. See Wee Yeow said that he could not bring himself to place his lips on those of Mohammed Hassan Yasi, because the patient's breath was disagreeable. Dr. Yeow claimed that Yasi, thirty-three, a Guyanan visiting relatives in Toronto, collapsed in his office after suffering an allergic reaction to a penicillin shot for a venereal disease. Dr. Yeow testified that he kept his mouth about a finger's width from Yasi's. Another witness, Jorge Maldana, testified that he helped with the mouth-to-mouth treatment, but stopped after a few minutes because of the "awful smell." George Atkinson, a driver-attendant with the Toronto department of ambulance services, told the inquest jury that resuscitation is almost impossible without mouth-to-mouth contact. (*Victoria, B.C. Times*)

A retired German army officer was hospitalized in Cologne as a result of skin infections caused by wearing military medals pinned to his naked chest. The officer served in the WW11 Wehrmacht and in the West German Bundeswehr and had reportedly found it difficult to adjust to civilian life. His wife told doctors that he wore the Iron Cross and similar decorations to bed and ran up the flag in their bedroom. (*Manila Philippines Times Journal*)

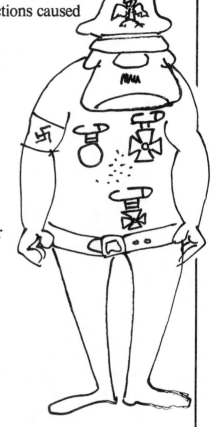

Ramon Rivera Rodriguez, a Venezuelan fisherman, woke up in his coffin, discovered that he was about to be buried, and immediately suffered a fatal heart attack. Witnesses say Rodriguez got out of the coffin in front of his grieving relatives and removed the cotton swabs from his nose; then, as his predicament became clear, he slumped to the ground and died. His relatives are seeking legal action against the doctor who had pronounced him dead the first time after he had a fit. (*Toronto Globe and Mail*)

I have never enjoyed eating, although I have been blessed with first a mother and then a wife who have been able to prepare meals the likes of which Benoit, Child, and Beard would swop their mothers for.

As to the quality of food, I can speak with some authority. Having paid $600 for a meal in one of the most expensive restaurants in the world, and having shared the eyes of a sheep with an Arab chief in the Negev desert, I can tell you from experience that both meals took the same route and were kicked and pounded by the same little army of stomach punchers on the way to the great outdoors once again.

Eating, like sleeping, is time consuming. The most valuable commodity known to man, time, is thrown to one side by the belching millions of gourmet tasters. Losers all.

Including the one being eaten ...

A twenty-six-year-old native of Dacca, Bangladesh, known as "cannibal Khalilullah," was arrested by the police after it was discovered that he had been eating corpses in a medical college morgue for three years.

A part-time reporter on a Bengali newspaper was keeping a close watch on the morgue. When the students left the room after a surgical demonstration, the reporter stated that he found Khalilullah eating the heart of a dissected corpse. According to his report, Khalilullah admitted to the craving. "I get the urge every two weeks or so, and then nothing can stop me," he said. It all started when he was twenty years old and developed what he confessed was an "intense attraction" for dead bodies. He said he was very active in removing bodies off the streets in 1971 during the bloodshed of the Bangladesh independence movement. Three years ago, Khalilullah volunteered to work as a "casual helper" in the Dacca medical college morgue, and had been having his macabre meals ever since.

(*London Times*)

A band of Cambodian soldiers, who were involved in a one-year siege and went four months without pay, killed a government paymaster when he showed up at their unit and ate him. Witnesses to the incident claimed that the soldiers' commander demanded back pay for his men from the paymaster, an officer of the army finance committee. When he had nothing to give them, the soldiers shot him, cut up his body, and ate him.

Using saws and kitchen knives, Japanese gangsters hacked Shoichi Murakami to small pieces in the back room of a Tokyo soup stall. The cook was subsequently forced to assist in destroying the victim's finger prints by boiling Murakami's severed hands as a base for the soup of the day. Of the fifty Japanese customers believed to have ordered it, none complained. (*Rafu Shimpo*)

A giant shark that was scheduled to be a delicacy in a fish market in Manila suddenly discouraged prospective buyers when a woman's head popped out of the fish's belly as it was cut open. The shark was the hammerhead variety and weighed about a ton. It had been captured by five fishermen of Cebu province. Deeper in the eighteen-foot-long beast's belly were human limbs and the remains of what looked like a dog. (*New York Post*)

I went into a shop intending to buy some cheese. Seeing some flies hovering around the uncovered cheese I spoke to the assistant and was surprised to be told, "They are fresh flies. They were not there yesterday." (*The Toronto Star*)

According to the Knight-Ridder News Service, the inscription on the metal bands used by the U.S. Department of the Interior to tag migratory birds has been changed. The bands used to bear the address of the Washington Biological Survey, abbreviated *Wash. Biol. Surv.* until the agency received the following letter from an Arkansas farmer:

"Dear Sirs: I shot one of your crows the other day. My wife followed the cooking instructions on the leg tag and I want to tell you it was horrible." The bands are now marked *Fish and Wildlife Service.*
(*Akron Beacon Herald*)

Every day for fifty years, Jeanette Gilbert
had afternoon tea in Robert Simon's cafe.
Simon observed the widow's eighty-fifth birthday
by promising her a free drink of her
choice every day for the rest of her life.
Although Mrs. Gilbert had never touched
liquor, she couldn't resist Simon's
birthday offer and ordered champagne and
assorted liqueurs.
Leaving the restaurant, she got the hiccups,
walked in front of a speeding truck, and
was killed. (*Times Picayune*)

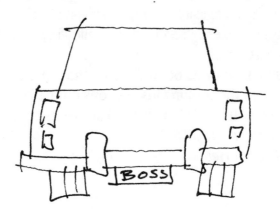

I hate cars.

Mind you, I don't understand cars. But there again, I don't understand women, yet I love them. So what is it about the car? For one thing, the oily, smelly tin box continues to be a complete mystery to me. How it runs? How it stops? Why it runs on gasoline and not water? Or why we buy them? Certainly, if God had meant us to drive, he would have given us a windshield wiper instead of a nose. No, I'm convinced that man began his downward rush toward the loser's paddock the day he chipped away at a rock and ended with a wheel. From a gentle, placid, plant-eating being, a monster was created – a cursing, fist-shaking ogre who would gladly run across the legs of a little old lady if she stood between him and a can of gas. Homo sapiens became an animal. Would you believe a camel?

When police arrived at the scene of a two-car collision in Ventura, California, they found a totally nude woman behind the wheel of one of the cars. The thirty-five-year-old Los Angeles resident was booked for investigation of reckless driving. She told officers that when she began her drive, she *thought* she was a camel in Morocco; but when she saw palm trees lining the downtown streets, she was convinced. (*San Francisco Chronicle*)

After a quarrel with his wife Shirley, Emerson Reed stormed out of the house. Thinking her husband was walking down the road, Shirley and several of their eight children piled into the family car after him. Shirley was backing the car down the driveway when the children screamed, "Mommy, you've run over Daddy." Emerson, who had been lying on the grass behind the car, tried to get up after a tire had run over his stomach. Shirley panicked and drove the car back up the driveway, running over her husband again. Emerson Reed managed to get up and comfort Shirley, who had by then dissolved into tears. Mr. Reed was hospitalized for observation, complaining that it was hard to catch his breath. (*Toledo, Ohio Blade*)

A series of excerpts from auto accident insurance claims filed by South African drivers was recently printed in a trade magazine published by an organization of South African accountants. Among the explanations offered by local drivers for accidents in which they were involved were:

"I consider neither vehicle was to blame, but if either was to blame it was the other one. The other car ran into mine without giving me any warning of its intention to do so."

"The other man altered his mind, so I had to run over him."

"A pedestrian hit me and went under the car."

"I thought the side window was down, but it was up ... as I found when I put my head through it."

"I collided with a stationary bus coming the other way."

"Coming home I drove into the wrong house and collided with a tree that I haven't got."

"My car had to turn sharper than necessary owing to an invisible truck."

"Sue suddenly saw me, lost her head, and we met sideways."

"One wheel went into the ditch, my feet jumped from the brake to the accelerator, leapt across the other side of the road, and jumped into the trunk of a tree." (*Idaho Statesman*)

Jose Manuel Martinez, thirty-three, of Gijon, Spain, ran out of luck last May. Martinez was thrown out of his car when it collided with another car in the town of Carreno. While he was lying unconscious on the road, he was run over by a passing truck. And, finally, a car which was taking him to a hospital overturned, killing him. According to the Spanish police, no one else was hurt in any of the accidents. (*New York Daily News*)

In Latina, Italy, Biagio di Crescenzo, twenty-three, crashed his car into a tree and was badly injured. A passing motorist drove him to the hospital at Fondi where doctors sent him to Rome in an ambulance for neurological treatment. The speeding ambulance hit an oncoming car. A passerby raced him to another hospital, where he was sent in yet another ambulance toward Rome. That ambulance skidded near Rome's outskirts and smashed into another car. Police said that the third accident killed di Crescenzo. (*Stars and Stripes*)

A car driven by Napoleon Gaithers left the road and struck a tree at a busy intersection in Winston-Salem, North Carolina. Two minutes later, another car went out of control and hit the same tree. It was driven by Gaithers's wife, Odessa. (*Raleigh (NC) News & Observer*)

Twenty-seven-year-old Carmon Leo complained that a rear-end auto collision turned him into a homosexual. Although his only physical injury was to his back, Leo said the accident had a jarring effect on his personality and altered his sexuality. The back injury kept him from work for six months, robbing him of his masculinity, Leo said. "When I found I couldn't function in the business world and support my wife, the effect was emasculating." According to his attorney, after the accident, Leo left his wife, moved in with his parents, and started hanging around gay bars and reading homosexual literature. The Wayne County Circuit Court jury awarded him $200,000. The jury also awarded his wife $25,000. (*Akron Beacon Journal*)

A dragline operator in Belle Glade, Florida, was so proud of his new 750 Honda that he invited a neighbour over to show off the machine. As the two men were standing on the patio admiring the motorcycle, the new owner pressed the electric starter button in order to prove how quietly the engine ran. The motorcycle was in gear, and plunged through a glass door into his living room, dragging him along with it. He was taken to the hospital, where he received treatment for numerous cuts on his arms and face. Meanwhile, his wife was sopping up gasoline that was leaking from the motorcycle, which was lying on its side in the living room. She flushed some gasoline-soaked paper towels down the toilet.

Her husband returned home from the hospital, saw his new motorcycle and the shattered patio door, and took shelter in his bathroom. He lit a cigarette and sat on the john, dropping the match into the toilet bowl. The paper towels had clogged the pipes, and the match detonated the gasoline. The explosion blew the commode to pieces and propelled the man into the air, inflicting third degree burns on his exposed underside.

His wife called for an ambulance. Because of the burns, the attendants had to carry him spread-eagle, face-down on the stretcher. As he was being carried inside the hospital, one of the attendants tripped, and the stretcher crashed to the ground. The fall left the owner of the new 750 Honda with a broken leg, amongst other things.

(*Palm Beach Post Times*)

In a recent startling rejection of the laws of probability, the following minor traffic incident took place in Prague, Czechoslovakia. An elderly man, ignoring a red pedestrian signal, rushed across a busy street. An oncoming car slammed on its brakes to avoid knocking him down, and went into a skid, whereupon the back door opened and a young girl holding a shopping bag fell out onto the street. A passerby who had observed the accident cried out and ran over to the car, which had landed undamaged at the curb. An old woman was crying in the back seat of the car. The careless elderly pedestrian turned out to be the father of the driver and of the girl who fell onto the street. The concerned passerby was another of his sons. The crying woman was his wife. No one was injured. (*New York Times*)

A twenty-two-year-old steel worker in Belfast, Northern Ireland, was hospitalized recently with a fractured skull, broken pelvis, broken leg, and other injuries after being struck by four vehicles within two minutes. Bob Finnegan was crossing the street when a taxi struck him and flung him over its roof. The taxi drove away, and, as Finnegan lay stunned in the road, a car ran into him, bowling him into the gutter. It, too, drove on. While pedestrians gathered at the scene, a small van ploughed through the crowd, leaving behind three injured bystanders and an even more battered Finnegan. When a fourth vehicle came along, the crowd scattered and only one man was hit – Finnegan.

Hospital officials say Finnegan will recover. (*Chicago Sun Times*)

A French motorist's Citroen stalled on a railroad crossing. Unable to move the car, he fled. A freight train hit the automobile, derailed, tore up 300 feet of track, and spilled twenty box cars loaded with beer into an adjacent river. Three cranes had to be rented to remove the remains of the freight train. Rail service was disrupted for six weeks. The beer killed all the fish in the river and put local fishermen out of work for the season. And the locomotive engineer sued for two cracked ribs. The total claim against the motorist's insurance company exceeded seven million dollars. (*Road and Track*)

Gaetano Regoli and Aristide Goffi were driving toward one another in thick fog on a narrow road in rural Italy. Both men leaned out their window in order to see better, and ended up in the hospital when they smacked their heads. (*National Observer*)

A one-legged, seventy-one-year-old woman in London got into her special invalid car, ran over her lodger, and then died when her car went out of control, burst into flames, and exploded. Police reported that Miss Esther O'Keefe of Dagenham, in northeast London, had a violent argument with her lodger, Miss Marion Marsh, thirty-nine. Miss Marsh left the house and went to a nearby park. Miss O'Keefe followed her in her specially-made, single seat, gasoline-driven invalid car. She chased her lodger for five miles before knocking her down. Two men lifted the car off Miss Marsh, but Miss O'Keefe sped off; then the car spun out of control, burst into flames, and blew up. Miss O'Keefe died of burns in a hospital. Miss Marsh was treated for shock and bruises. (*Vancouver Sun*)

Angry bus patrons in the Midlands of England complained to bus company officials when drivers repeatedly failed to stop and pick them up. They claimed operators would sometimes smile and wave as they drove by. In defence, the company noted, "It is impossible for the drivers to keep their timetable if they have to stop for passengers." (*Campus Life*)

"Sticks and stones may break my bones but words will never harm me."

Don't you believe it. There are few things in life more damaging than the verbal put down. To be reminded that one has entered the loser's stable is to hear a cutting remark circle a room and wallop its way smack between your eyes. The verbal put down strikes at the very heart of a loser's make-up – his intellect or lack of it. The names of those wits who have used their words like a shipyard docker would use his boots are legendary. Oscar Wilde, Dorothy Parker, Winston Churchill, Charles Lamb, Jonathan Swift . . . I could go on and on. But here are a few, together with the losers as recorded at the scene of the battles.

Dame Edith Evans was told that Nancy
Mitford had been lent a villa so that
she could finish a book:

> "OH REALLY. WHAT
> EXACTLY IS SHE
> READING?"

Margot Asquith, wife of the English
Liberal Prime Minister, once made a
visit to Hollywood where she was
introduced to Jean Harlow. The movie
star had not encountered the name
"Margot" before and asked if the
"t" was pronounced or not.

> "NO. THE 't' IS SILENT –
> AS IN HARLOW."

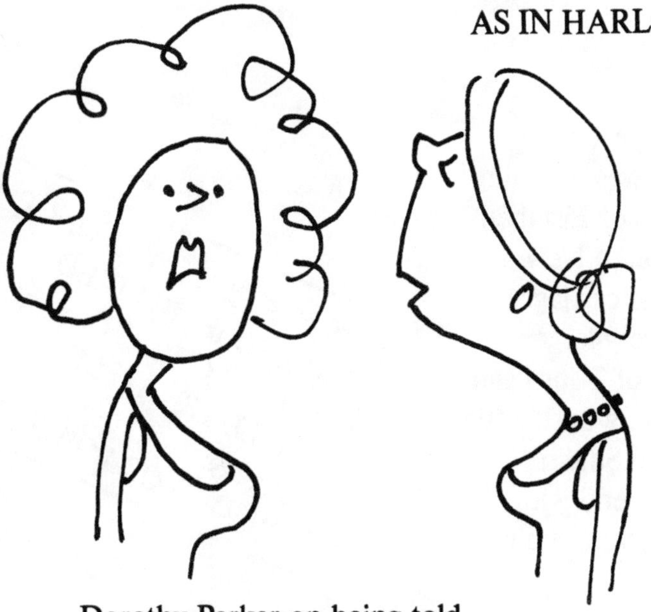

Dorothy Parker on being told
that Coolidge was dead, remarked:

> "HOW CAN YOU TELL?"

Groucho Marx was going down in the elevator at the Hotel Danieli in Venice. At the fourth floor a group of priests got in. One of them recognized Groucho and said, "Excuse me Mr. Marx, but my mother was a great fan of yours."
To which Groucho retorted;

"I DIDN'T KNOW YOU GUYS WERE ALLOWED TO HAVE MOTHERS."

Noel Coward was watching the coronation of Elizabeth II on television in New York when the carriage carrying the very large Queen Salote of Tonga came into view. Sitting beside the Queen was the Sultan Kelantan. A friend with Coward asked who the man was:

"HER LUNCH," answered Coward.

W.C. FIELDS WAS ONCE ASKED IF HE LIKED LITTLE CHILDREN. FIELDS SNAPPED BACK: "FRIED OR BOILED?"

The British conductor, Sir Thomas Beecham, was travelling in the no smoking carriage of a train when a woman passenger lit a cigarette and asked, "You won't object if I smoke?"

To which Beecham replied, "Certainly not – and you won't object if I'm sick."

It was in the days when the railways were still privately owned. "I don't think you know who I am," the woman angrily pointed out. "I am one of the director's wives."

To which Beecham replied:

"MADAM" IF YOU WERE THE DIRECTOR'S ONLY WIFE, I SHOULD STILL BE SICK."

Shaw sent Churchill two tickets for the first night of *St. Joan*, "One for yourself, one for a friend – if you have one."

Churchill expressed regret at not being able to attend and replied by requesting tickets for the second night.

"IF THERE IS ONE."

Who is a winner and who is a loser and who has the answer?
For many it is Hollywood. "This person is beautiful and
will be the toast of the town, that one is a loser and needs
a face job." Anxious to hide whatever defects the film
capital decrees as ugly, men and women gallop for the
beauty and drug stores to buy the muck and crap that will
hide the face of the loser that stares back at them from the
bathroom mirror. If only they knew. Beauty is in the eye
of the beholder, and most fans need glasses. Their heroes
have all had defects. And if a defect is the sign of a loser
– here are a few of the lesser known losers and their
defects.

Big Ears

Rudolph Valentino
Had two beauties of the cauliflower variety.
Fortunately for the lustre-haired sex symbol a friend was
highly skilled in the gentle art of cosmetic camouflage.

Guglielmo Marconi
Came into the world with a pair of enormous ears.
"Ah, but he will be able to hear the still, small
voice of the air," said his mother.

And what about the ears of Albert Camus, Martha Graham,
Lizzie Borden, Pope John, Georges Enesco, Jonas Salk
and Clark Gable?
All distinctly odd.
And lest we forget;
Fred Astaire:

Large Noses

Rudolf of Hapsburg
Had a nose so big that
artists were afraid to
paint its full dimension.

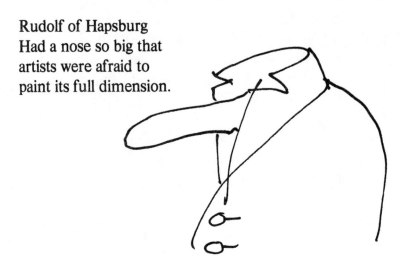

Bishop Of Ely
In reporting the Bishop's escape to the continent from an
English charge of treason, Lord Macaulay, the historian,
snidely expressed surprise
that the Bishop could have
travelled unnoticed, "for his
nose was such as none who had
seen it could ever forget."

The French Duke of Anjou
A rejected suitor of Queen Elizabeth had a king-size nose
as Dr. Cooke-Taylor rhymed:
    Good people of Flanders pray do not suppose
    It is monstrous this Frenchman should double his nose,
    Dame nature her favors but merely misplaces,
    She had given two noses to match his two faces.

Large Feet and No Feet

George Washington
Was always embarrassed by his big feet.

Peter Stuyvesant
Had a leg injured during a battle in Venezuela.
Returned home to Holland and had an artificial
leg made for himself complete with silver
trimmings.

Prince Frederick of Hamburg
Lost a leg in battle and went one further than
Peter. He had a silver leg made.

Prince Frederick III of Germany
Kicked in a door so hard in a fit of temper
that he had to have it amputated.

Hegisistratus
A Greek seer. He was held prisoner by the Spartans
who decided to chain his leg to the floor to stop
him escaping. Hegisistratus had other ideas. Unable
to pick the lock he did the next best thing. Cut off
his leg and made it back home, thirty miles away.
He was so mad at the Spartans that he waited for the
wound to heal, made himself a wooden leg, and then got
back to chasing them again.

No Hands

Sir Robert R
When serving with the English army in Scotland, the sexy old Lord seduced a local girl who had a very irritable brother. The enraged man joined Sir Robert's regiment the day before the Battle of Culloden and ignored both the enemy and his own army. He decided to zero in on Sir Robert and hack off his hand.

CHARGE!

Lord Nelson
Was constantly waving his arms around during the height of battle. Not surprisingly, a cannon ball fired during a sea fight at Tenerife promptly relieved him of one. Not that it bothered him all that much. Two days later he was busy writing letters again with his other hand.

Horuk Barbarossa
A Turkish pirate lost his hand during a fight with the Spaniards. From then on he wore an iron hand up to his elbow. "Very useful in winning battles," he claimed.

No Hair

Caesar
Sang proudly of his bald head
thinking it was a mark of his
virility.

I'M IN THE MOOD FOR LOVE

Louis XIII
Bald by the age of twenty-three was so embarrassed by his
bald top that he wore a wig even though the thinking in
the middle ages was that baldness was thought to be a sign
of the devil.

Elisha
Was walking down a road minding his own business when
a group of ruffian children began to call after him
screaming, "Go down thou Bald Pate." Justice was swift
in those times. We're told that a bear, on hearing the
noise, rushed from the woods and ate forty-two of them.

Louis XIV
Refused to be seen without his wig. Even the valet was
forced to pass the hair
pieces through the royal
curtains of the king's
bed.

No Hair

Queen Elizabeth I and William
Shakespeare, Yul Brynner and Telly Savalas.

So you're a loser.
You feel you could have
made the above list.
Think positive:

Don Herold,
the American humorist,
had the right idea.
"There's one thing
about baldness, it's neat."

Okay. So you'd still rather
have hair on top:

King Chatos of Egypt
Bald as an egg had a mother who set out to cure his
problem with a concoction of dogs' paws, dates, and
asses' hooves.

Hippocrates
Had a basic answer. A salve of opium, roses or lilies.
Wine and unripe olive oil.
For more serious add pigeon droppings and horse radish.

and remember:

66

Mary Queen of Scots
Lost her head on February 8, 1587. The executioner, who had already had three tries at removing the Queen's head finally succeeded. He then lifted the head to show the crowd only to have it fall to the ground leaving him holding the wig of Mary high in the air.

Anne Boleyn
Lost her head on May 20, 1536. Within a fortnight, her widowed Henry VIII took a new wife. Anne's only chance to miss death was to bear Henry a son. She may have done this had she not caught Henry playing about with a Lady-in-Waiting. The result of the shock caused her to have a miscarriage.

Marie Antoinette

Lost her head to the guillotine in 1793. As she made her way to the block she turned to face the executioner, a fellow by the name of Samson, and promptly stepped on his foot.

Charles I

Lost his head on January 30, 1649, after a falling out with Oliver Cromwell. The poor king had to wait four hours before stepping onto the platform. "What shall I do with my hair?" he asked the axeman. It was decided that it would be best if he tucked it under the nightcap he was wearing. His head was off in a single stroke. A spectator commented, "There was such a groan by the thousands present as I never heard before and desire I may never hear again."

Poor Eyes or No Eyes

Theodore Roosevelt
Before riding up San Juan Hill stuffed every pocket with
spare pairs of glasses just in case one of them were shot off.

Lord Nelson
Lost an eye in battle. Although many paintings of
England's greatest Admiral show him wearing an eye
patch, he never did. What he did wear was a special shade
fixed to his hat to protect his good eye from the glare of
the sun. His blind eye was saved for special occasions,
such as the battle of Copenhagen. Signalled to break off
the action, Nelson took a telescope from an officer and
put it to his blind eye. "I really do not see the signal," he
remarked to the astonished man.

Henry VIII
Owned ten pair of glasses which certainly
blows the lid on his sight problem. We're
told he paid 4 d. apiece for them.

Zachary Taylor
Was so short sighted that he had to squint an eye to read. He also had great difficulty getting his hands in his pockets. When a letter arrived telling him that he'd been nominated for Vice President Zachary missed getting the news since he turned away the messenger when he was told that there was extra money to pay for the postage.

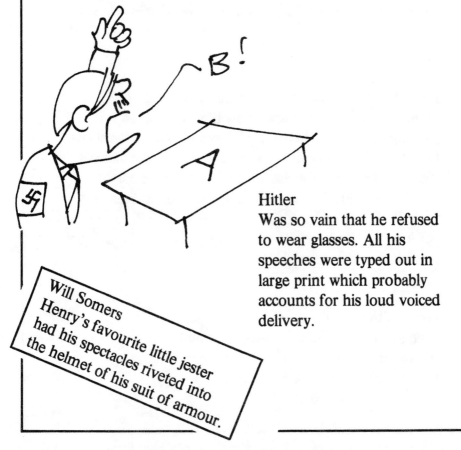

Hitler
Was so vain that he refused to wear glasses. All his speeches were typed out in large print which probably accounts for his loud voiced delivery.

Will Somers
Henry's favourite little jester had his spectacles riveted into the helmet of his suit of armour.

Loser Tall and Losers Short

Francis Zunega
A dwarf in the service of Charles V of Spain was so witty that he was expelled from the court hoping that this would shut him up. It didn't. He continued to wise-crack and was finally stabbed in an effort to gag him. It did the trick but not before the one last remark. Perico de Ayold, a friend of the dwarf asked the dying Francis to pray for him when he got to heaven. Back came the reply. "Okay, tie a string around my finger so I don't forget."

Sir Jeffrey Hudson
Was a captain of the horse in the service of Charles I. At 3 foot 9 inches in height was probably the smallest knight in history. Once caught a large nobleman making faces in his direction and decided to take the smile off the fellow's face by challenging him to a duel of swords. Took the smile and the big man's life from him.

The largest number of losers in this book will be found under this heading of Crime. It would seem that the more the human being becomes involved with the shady side of life, the more he or she is likely to commit an act that brands them with the large "L." And as if the act itself were not proof enough, many continue to gather loser points long after the initial act is over.

Lack of freedom can cause people to do astonishing things, like acquiring an appetite for the strangest of food.

Hannes Schaarschmidt was so desperate to escape from a German prison in 1907 that he ate himself out. Each day the prisoner chewed away at the heavy wooden bars; then to avoid suspicion, he filled the holes made by his teeth with a paste made of the black bread supplied to the prisoners. After three months Hannes was able to squeeze through and make a run for it. Unfortunately he was caught within three weeks and this time found himself in a cell with iron bars.

When the sheriff at the Marshall County jail in Iowa shoved trays full of delicious TV dinners under the cell doors, the boys just shoved them straight back again. Said one inmate in a fit of righteous indignation: "We're not going to eat that slop."

For the girls of Champaign University, Illinois, in 1977, it was standing room only in the washrooms as females by the dozen fell victim to the "Enema Bandit." The villain would sneak into the girls' dorm, tie up a resident, and forcibly give her an enema. He was eventually "flushed out" and prosecuted.

In 1978 Cora Draper of Crystal Beach beat her husband to death with his artificial arm. The mother of six was sentenced to three years in prison after her lawyer claimed that she had been provoked by insults from her husband and that they were both drunk at the time. Mr. Draper was not wearing his arm during the incident.

Speaking about a sixteen-year-old-boy who was accused of offences against two girls, Mr. Stephen Coates, a psychologist, said at Luton Juvenile Court: "Previously he has been found guilty of offences which suggested a homosexual nature. These latest offences are at least a step in the right direction." (*News Of The World*)

Edward John Brookes of Spring Lane, England, was sent to prison for eighteen months by the Crown Court at Aylesbury after he pleaded guilty to stealing 35,683 broom handles. (*Buckingham Advertiser*)

William A. Fugua of Fort Worth, Texas was standing perfectly still in his role as a live mannequin when he was stabbed in the back by a man trying to prove to his wife that Fugua was real.

Colin Rich, twenty-seven and unemployed, tried to live up to his name but it just wasn't his day. His first mistake was donning three stocking masks and a scarf as he entered a London, Ontario, bank he planned to stick up. His disguise kept customers and employees from seeing his face – but it also kept him from seeing them. He blundered around the bank for a while
and then decided it was time
to pull out a weapon and
get on with the job. He
reached in his pocket
and pulled out
a glasses
case.
When caught
by the
police he was hiding
behind a car outside the bank.

When Lorenzo Castelli was struck and killed by a train the Italian railroad sued him on charges of delaying rail schedules for twenty-nine minutes.

After visiting his lawyer, Ernesto Battisti of Latina, Italy, was abducted by two men. When police gave chase the two men hurled poor Ernesto out of the speeding car. Police took him to the local police station to help him recover from the shock of his ordeal. They then arrested him on fraud charges connected with his wholesale meat business. The kidnappers escaped.

A man who was hanging on the coat rack at Burnham police station and broke it was fined $250 by Burnham magistrates on Monday. (*Slough Express*)

Bandits trying to break into an office in Rome for a payroll robbery even went so far as to fire a submachine-gun burst at the lock, but still did not manage to get inside. Finally, they gave up and fled. Police said they had been pulling at the door instead of pushing. (*San Jose News*)

Michael Fry and Kenneth Harris work in a Chicago gas station. Three gunmen entered the gas station early one morning, tied them up, and helped themselves to $5,000 from the station safe and $390 worth of cigarettes. The robbers fled, leaving Fry and Harris bound and gagged on the floor. During the time they were tied up, the attendants said the station had a steady stream of customers. They looked in, saw the pair helpless on the floor, and then proceeded to take cigarettes and fill their tanks with gasoline. After two hours of this free-for-all, one customer phoned police, although he did not leave his name because he was in the process of filling up his gas tank. Authorities estimate that 100 drivers took part in the freebies. (*New York Daily News*)

After Roberto Tercero reported that he had been robbed, police routinely questioned him in hopes of discovering the thief's identity. When asked if Tercero had noticed anything unusual about the robber's appearance, he replied, "He had popsicle sticks up his nose, grey socks on his hands, and he wore a brown paper bag as a hat." No arrests have as yet been made. (*New York Daily News*)

ARE YOU SURE IT'S HIM?

Larry Burnstin was arrested for standing nude on a street corner in San Francisco. The charges were dismissed for lack of evidence, whereupon Burnstin walked out into the courtroom hall and dropped his pants. Burnstin explained that he was "merely expressing his joy." He was booked for indecent exposure. (*Toronto Star*)

Filbert Maestas, of Colorado, stole a number of cardboard cartons from a meat packing plant there, presuming that they contained frozen cuts of beef. The packages were actually filled with 1,200 cow rectums. Maestas was convicted of theft, but appealed on the grounds that the police had laughed at him in order to extract a confession. According to the court records, the arresting officer had said to Maestas. "You won't believe what you took ... 1,200 beef assholes!"
Maestas is reported to have replied. "If I go to jail for stealing beef assholes, I'm really going to be mad."
The Colorado Court of Appeals let the conviction stand. (*Rocky Mountain News*)

Winfield S. Waters, an eighty-five-year-old man served five years of a life sentence for the attempted rape of a school teacher, before being ordered freed by Federal Judge Alexander Harvey III. Federal authorities said the octogenarian could not have attempted the rape because of his age, his near blindness, and the crippled condition of his legs. (*Philadelphia Bulletin*)

A judge in the Philippines, angered by increasing crime, has recommended a number of new punishments to deter it, including skinning criminals alive and spraying them with vinegar until they die. (*St. Louis Post-Dispatch*)

Arrested on charges of malicious mischief, Mr. Frank E. Taylor, eighty-six, of Hollywood, used his one free telephone call to contact Los Angeles International Airport and make a bomb threat.

The Plainfield, New Jersey, police report that a burglar kicked in the rear door of Mrs. Wilma Barnett's home and stole a television set, the kitchen clock, and Mrs. Barnett's full-grown German shepherd watchdog.

Samuel Eastman told Nassau County police that when he and his wife returned home from a night out, he found a stranger having a drink and talking to his collie. The man told him that "the dog invited me in and asked me to join him in a drink. So I poured a Scotch for him and one for myself." Eastman called the police, and the stranger, Douglas Cameron, a twenty-nine-year-old market researcher, was charged with burglary. The case then went to a grand jury, which refused to indict Cameron. (*Boston Globe*)

Maria Marcon, twenty-four, of Rome, Italy, got off a train and accepted a ride from a dark-haired stranger. Shortly after she entered the car, a three-foot dwarf popped out of a cardboard box on the back seat, clubbed her over the head, and stole $60 from her purse. When she came to, she was lying on the street. (*Canadian Press*)

One morning in May, an insurance salesman on his way to work on Wall Street was standing near the open doors of a New York subway car that had stopped at a station, when a short, well-dressed man entered the car, bumped into him, then abruptly left again. The insurance salesman instinctively felt for his wallet and, finding it missing, reached out and grabbed the short man by his jacket collar. The subway doors closed with their rubber edges around the salesman's wrists, but he held on even after the car started moving, and managed to drag the other man several feet along the station platform before the material of the man's jacket tore, leaving him holding a few inches of tweed in his hands. Ten minutes after the insurance salesman reached his office, still fuming at the incident, his wife called to tell him that he had left his wallet at home. (*New York Times*)

At 7.00 o'clock on Tuesday morning, Margret Radovich, fifty, of Homewood, Illinois, shot her husband Theodore, fifty-six, twice in the chest while he slept. Some time later she got into the bed herself and fell asleep. Theodore regained consciousness about 3.00 AM on Wednesday and finding his wife next to him, pulled the gun out of her hand and shot her once in each leg. He then attempted to throw the gun out a window, but it fell back into the room. Mrs. Radovich found and reloaded the gun. While Mr. Radovich crawled into another part of the house, she crawled after him and shot him in the mouth. He managed to crawl away, and she then shot herself while he broke a window and called for help. Police found Mrs. Radovich on the floor, but before they could reach her she took one more shot at her husband. The shot missed and she fell, dead. (*Newsday*)

A workman was recently shot to death by police in the Mexican town of Coacalco. Four thousand angry towns-people determined the killing should not have taken place, and subsequently mobbed the mayor's office to obtain justice. They forced the mayor to eat twelve pounds of bananas and resign. (*Tucson Citizen*)

A Fordham University co-ed tried to dissuade a would-be rapist by telling him she was a homosexual. In further conversation, the attacker admitted that he, too, was a homosexual. The woman then informed him she knew of a dormitory guard who was homosexual, and upon her suggestion, the man abandoned his rape attempt and went off to look for the guard. He was later arrested on charges of attempted sodomy, attempted robbery, and sexual abuse. (*Wilmington Evening Journal*)

A forty-three-year-old masked bandit held up a gas station with dog feces, instructing attendants to empty the till lest they be forced to eat a handful. Ninety dollars was surrendered and the robber departed. A police dog tracked him down in less than an hour. (*Province*)

Police in Oakland, California, spent two hours attempting to subdue a gunman who had sealed himself inside his home. After firing ten tear gas canisters, officers discovered the man was standing beside them shouting pleas to himself to come out of the house and give himself up. He was placed in a psychiatric hospital. (*Newsday*)

A vandal in South London has smashed twenty brick walls into dust for no apparent reason. The prowler, nicknamed "Harvey Wallbanger" by police, roams the streets after dark in search of garden walls, and then uses a sledgehammer to demolish them. "Perhaps it's a bricklayer who is finding it difficult to get work," suggested one victim. (*Toronto Star*)

An attempted holdup of a branch of the Marine Midland Bank in Buffalo, New York, was thwarted by a persistent teller. According to Lieut. Raymond Fries of the Buffalo police, a man approached the teller, who had been held up several times before, and said, "I've got a gun. Hand over the money."
"Show me the gun," insisted the teller.
"I can't," replied the would-be holdup man. "Other people in the bank would see it."
"Well, then give me a note," said the teller.
"Give me a piece of paper," said the holdup man.
The teller handed him a piece of paper. While he was writing a note, another teller leaned over and asked what was going on. At that point, the holdup man threw up his hands and said, "Oh, the hell with it," and ran out of the bank.
He was captured by the police a block away.(*New York Times*)

A twenty-one-year-old Japanese student was arrested in Tokyo when he was found loitering in a residential district with women's panties in his trouser pockets. Toshihito Sakai told police that he couldn't resist stealing women's underwear. One thousand five hundred undergarments were subsequently found in his apartment.

An unusual shoplifting incident occurred in London, England, during the last Christmas season. A little old lady collapsed in a supermarket, and was subsequently diagnosed by an ambulance attendant as suffering from extreme cold. She was found to have hidden a frozen chicken under her large, veiled hat. (*Los Angeles Times*)

In an attempt to cut down on airplane hijacking, one enterprising airline recently hired two psychiatrists as special security officers. The two men were instructed to arrest anyone who showed signs of mental instability. Within minutes of their first spell of duty, one of the psychiatrists arrested the other. (*Police Journal*)

Vincent Johnson and Frazier Black walked into an Austin bank and tried to cash a $200 check. It was made out to a Nancy Hart. They had her deposit slip, too, and they wanted half the sum deposited in her account, and half in cash. The check was forged, and the deposit slip stolen; but no one would have known except for one small thing. The teller they approached was Nancy Hart. "It was a one in a million chance occurrence," said a detective. "If I never solve another case, this one makes it worth it." (*Wichita Eagle*)

Labourer Graham Loft, of Gravesend, was fined $25 by the town's magistrate for smashing a window at Chalmers Wholesale, King Street, with a brick. He said he threw it in the air hoping to drop it gently on his friend's foot. (*Rochester Evening Post*)

The magistrates were told that the strongest evidence against the defendant was that when he was being examined and being put through various tests to see if he was drunk, he was asked to clench his teeth, "whereupon he took them out and gave them to the divisional surgeon and said 'here, you clench them.'" (*Woking Herald*)

A police officer in Brooklyn, New York, accidentally shot himself in the leg after dropping his pants and gunbelt in the station's men's washroom.

The boy had listed among his fifty-two convictions, burglary, theft, malicious wounding, killing animals in a pet shop, and setting fire to a railway station. All the offences were committed before the boy was fifteen. But a social worker told magistrates, "These kids would not have such a bad record if the police would not keep arresting them." (*Sheffield Star*)

After grabbing the loot a bank robber in North Arlington vaulted over the bank counter and shot his finger off accidentally with his own gun. He made his getaway but police took a print from the finger and arrested him shortly after.

A shopkeeper in England found that thieves had got away with two mens' jackets from his Ipswich store. They hooked them off the display rack and pulled them through the letter box. (*Ipswich Evening Star*)

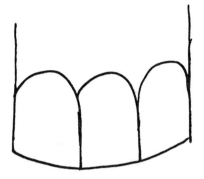

When I was a boy, it was said that in Petticoat Lane
Market, in London, England, sparrows were caught at
one end of the market, sprayed with gold paint, and sold
as canaries at the other end of the market. Whenever I've
thought about animal losers I've thought about those
sparrows. It tells the complete story. Most animals would
continue to be winners and never be losers except for the
intrusion on their world by humans. Which animal in his
right mind would want to take a trip to the local pub and
have a drink if it wasn't for the fact that his master was
feeling thirsty?

A regular drinker in Scotland explained how his best friend behaves when they are out for the evening. "Sometimes when out with Tonersson, the dog drank as many as eleven pints. The dog drinks beer until he gets fed up. Then he usually nudges me with his head when he wants whiskey." (*Scotsman*)

Cows which are allowed to roam the busy streets of London should be given a coat of luminous paint, an MP said today. (*Manchester Evening News*)

Dog lover Jerry Lewis discovered that his aging cocker spaniel was going deaf so he called in a group of electronic engineers and had them build a high frequency, solar battery powered canine hearing aid. Unfortunately the dog died and Jerry never did find out if the $15,000 hearing aid worked. (*Toronto Star*)

The sobering fact that available zoo statistics indicate that one elephant keeper has died for every calf elephant sired in a European zoo inspired Dr. Russell Jones, a research fellow at the London Zoo, to develop a method of inseminating female elephants without the need to directly involve a male or bull elephant, which is always a difficult beast to handle and at mating times is actually murderous.

Dr. Jones recently completed an African safari during which he devised a technique for obtaining elephant semen from bulls in the wild for eventual artificial insemination in females. His key equipment consisted of a large, custom-built aluminum probe and a twelve-volt car battery. After drugging the bull elephant by shooting it with a special dart rifle, Dr. Jones and his staff placed hats

on the immobilized elephants' heads to shield their eyes from the sun during the operation, and then inserted the aluminum probe into the animal's rectum, attached the car battery to the probe, and sent a hefty electrical shock into its reproductive tract. About a liter of sperm was produced in this manner.

The sperm is preserved by mixing it with egg yolk, freezing it with liquid nitrogen, and placing it in plastic straws developed in France for storing bull semen. When it comes time to inseminate a female, the straws will be thawed out and fired into a female's uterus through a special polyethylene tube. (*London Times*)

The world of bull-fighting is in a turmoil. According to veterinarian Luis Pomar, "Support for bull-fighting is at an all-time low." He claims that the promoters are using immature and inferior bulls. Indeed things have got so bad at one stadium that the matador was led off in tears when a bull laid down in the middle of the ring and fluttered its eyes at him. (*Toronto Star*)

M. Henri Villette of Alençon, France, decided to drown his cat. The elderly gentleman went down to the river Sarthe, gave a mighty heave, and flung the animal into the water. In doing so, M. Villette lost his balance, fell in, and drowned.
The cat swam back to land. (*New York News*)

Judge Robert Lymbery rejected an order that a 168-pound Great Dane be destroyed because it was dangerous. The English magistrate then gave the dog a friendly pat. The animal bit his hand twice. (*Atlanta Journal*)

I have a pet Budgerigar, which has a swing in its cage. I have made a practice of disconnecting this swing each Sunday and not returning it to the cage until Monday morning. Is this in accord with strict Christian principle? (*Belfast News*)

At a conference sponsored by the Church of Scientology, Victor Marchetti, former CIA executive assistant and a fourteen-year veteran with the agency, revealed that the CIA had once recruited a cat. In an attempt to eavesdrop on conversations held by enemy agents discussing covert plots against the American government, the animal was wired for sound. A problem arose, however. The cat developed hunger pangs and began wandering away from the target in search of food. Two new wires were implanted in the feline – one to detect the cat's hunger response, and another to abort it.

This didn't solve all of the CIA's problems. The cat was a tabby with an eye for the ladies, and tended to disappear in search of the opposite sex. So two more wires were implanted, one to detect the cat's sexual urges, and another to somehow bypass them.

After exhaustive testing, the cat was finally ready for its first assignment. It was turned loose in the street, followed by a CIA support truck loaded with electronic monitoring gear. The cat was immediately run over by a taxi cab. (*Springfield Advocate*)

While spectators stood terror struck, a gorilla
at a fair in Huddersfield, England, bent its
iron bars apart and charged the audience.
One brave man in the crowd grabbed an iron
bar and struck the beast over the head.
Unfortunately it wasn't a gorilla.
It was a stunt man, Mike
Towell, in a gorilla suit.
A news dispatch
from Huddersfield said,
"Police want to question
the would-be hero, who
was last seen running from
the tent pursued by Mr. Towell, who had blood
streaming from a head wound that required six
stitches." (*Boston Globe*)

Columbian children's television star Marco Polo was
acquitted of murder charges by an appeals court after the
eight-inch tall defendant allegedly bit an elderly woman to
death. Marco Polo is a monkey. Following a brief term in
jail with thirty-five prostitutes, the animal was tried and
sentenced to death. An attorney appealed the verdict and
the court released him to the custody of a zoo. (*Toronto
Star*)

The owners of a wildlife preserve in Winston, Oregon are desperately searching for a female companion for George, a two-humped camel who is so frustrated sexually that he has tried to mate with a fifteen-passenger minibus. "He works up a good frothing at the mouth and makes clumsy, lunging, drooling passes at the park's minibus every time it passes through his territory," says an official at the Wildlife Safari, George's home. George is twenty-seven years old, the equivalent of about ninety human years. (*Daily Record*)

An elderly South African woman was hospitalized in serious condition after vandals attacked her. Investigators later discovered the weapon – a stray Pomeranian dog dropped on her head from thirteen stories above. The weapon died. (*Reuters*)

John MacKay was fined $54 by an English court for assaulting, imprisoning, and torturing a parrot. Drunk, and disturbed by his bird's shrieking, MacKay forced the creature into a freezer, and later transferred it to an oven. He set the burner on a low heat. The parrot recovered after medical treatment, and was remanded to the care of Mrs. MacKay. (*Reuters*)

It was 1946. The war in Europe was over. Once again the finest singers in the world were making their way to London. One of the great Italian tenors, Beniamino Gigli, was appearing at the Albert Hall, accompanied by his own pianist. Tickets were at a premium. The hall was packed to such an extent that chairs had been set up on the stage – the ultimate honour for a visiting artist. I was lucky to find myself beside the pianist. It was an evening I will never forget. Gigli was magnificent. When the concert ended, Gigli and his pianist were called back for encores. After six more songs it did not seem possible that he would be able to make it back to centre stage again. Surely he would be exhausted. Standing with the others, I watched fascinated as, backstage, the pianist voiced his objections. Suddenly the accompanist sat on the floor. Gigli took one of his arms and dragged the limp pianist to the centre of the stage. The hall was in an uproar. On reaching the piano, Gigli lifted the pianist to the piano stool. He sang one more aria and was gone. One of the greatest tenors the world has ever seen and a reluctant pianist. A pianist who lost an argument to a singer. He was lucky. He could have had a piece of scenery hit him on the head.

Giorgio Tozzi stood on the stage of the Metropolitan
Opera house giving it his best shot during a performance
of Mozart's "The Magic Flute" when a piece of scenery
fell on his head. Luckily for Giorgio
a hefty wig he was wearing took most
of the damage.

Leo Slezak, the great Viennese tenor,
was belting out an aria in Lohengrin
when he turned to discover that the
swan-boat into which he had to climb
had been towed off the stage
without him. Not one to keep
a secret, Leo turned to the
nearest member of the chorus
and in a loud voice asked,
"When does the next swan leave?"

When tenor Carlo Bergonzi let loose a particularly
thin-voiced rendition of Celeste Aida at La Scala
the audience did more than tell him to go home. They threw
what was for them the ultimate insult. "You sound
like Frank Sinatra," they screamed.

Eva Cummings was the star soprano of an 1880's
troupe called the Milan Grand Italian Opera Company.
They had been booked to play Chicago and Eva was
performing her favourite role, the lead in Lucia
di Lammermoor. Things were going great until the
third act. The curtain went up. No Eva. The audience
became restless. Finally the curtain was lowered
and out stepped Signor Alberto Sarata, the manager
of the company. He was halfway through explaining
how sick Eva was and how she was unable to continue
when out from the curtains stepped an extremely
healthy looking Eva. She stood beside Alberto and
explained how she had never felt better and if she
was suffering any pain at all it was in the area of
her pocket. What she wanted, explained Eva, was some
hard-earned cash.
The audience were divided.
Half were cheering for Eva and half for the manager.
Not wishing to miss an opportunity to capture all
the votes Eva began to take bows. First to one
side of the theatre and then to the other.

In the meantime Alberto had sneaked off stage. Eva began to follow suit when to her horror she found the curtains being held fast. Unable to make it off one side of the stage Eva belted to the other side. Closed.

By now her smile was gone and the bowing had been replaced by a figure dashing from side to side. Suddenly, with a tremendous shout, Eva charged the centre of the curtains. The drapes held for a moment, then finally gave way sending poor Eva sprawling backstage.

Maria Jeritza and Enrico Caruso
once appeared together in a
production of the opera "Carmen"
at New York's Metropolitan Opera
House. No expense was spared with
real horses being used to pull the
coach carrying Carmen and
Escamillo onto the stage in the final
act. Nervous at such an occasion
one of the horses was unable to
contain himself and expressed his
stage fright in a rather distasteful
manner. Soon after this display of
nerves Caruso was called upon to
stab Jeritza. Maria refused to fall.
Caruso stabbed her for a second
time and screamed, "Die, fall, will
you."
Back came the reply.
"I'll die if you can find me a clean
place."

A singer named Waldick Soriano was singing a song called "I am not a dog" at an outdoor concert in Juazeiro Do Norte, Brazil, when a dog walked on stage wearing a sign that read "I'm not Waldick Soriano." Soriano was not amused and proceeded to insult the audience. A brawl resulted, and the singer fled to his hotel. (*Detroit Free Press*)

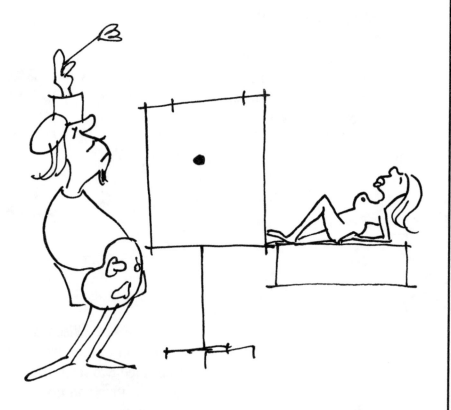

I myself attended one of the finest art schools in the world
– the Camberwell School of Art in London, England. I
went for exactly two weeks ... evening classes. It is some
measure of the school's efficiency that the teacher took so
little time deciding that I had no talent for the world of
paint sloshers known as artists. To this day, I feel a sense
of embarrassment every time I sell a drawing.
Nevertheless, I continue to cash the cheques. My only
regret is that I failed to reach the plateau known as life
study. However, it would appear that such painting can
cause the artist problems.

Zeuxis, the Greek painter, completed a portrait of an old lady in the year 397 B.C. and found the brush work so bad that he began chuckling to himself. Within minutes his chuckling had become uncontrollable and he laughed himself to death.

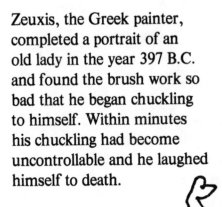

In Milwaukee, Wisconsin, a man and woman were each fined $75 for too much panting and not enough painting. Police, who were called to investigate a report of a possible break-in at an empty house, found the couple making love in the bedroom. The two had been hired to paint the building. Because they were not married they were charged with lewd and lascivious conduct. (*AP*)

Michelangelo's painting in the Sistine Chapel is magnificent but only he knows the problems involved when painting on a ceiling. It's a hell of a long way from the "roller and stick" method as he explained in the following sonnet:

I've grown a goitre by dwelling in this den ...
That drives the belly close beneath the chin:
My beard turns up to heaven; my nape falls in,
Fixed on my spine: my breastbone visibly
Grows like a harp: a rich embroidery
Bedews my face from brush-drops thick and thin ...

At last. An answer to the losers – prayer. From loser to winner all in one jump. A drop on to the knees and its back on the rails toward the chequered flag.

Enraged when a passerby gave him only a tiny amount of money, Raphael Santos, a Brazilian beggar, proceeded to beat the man with his crutch. By the time the police arrived, both men were surrounded by a large crowd, which was shouting, "A miracle! A miracle!" (*Private Eye*)

Florence Moffett of Detroit, Michigan, was asleep in her apartment when a man crawled through the bedroom window and attempted to sexually assault her. Ms. Moffett demanded that the man first allow her to read some passages from the Bible lying on her night stand. They discussed religion for several minutes and the man said that he had gone to Sunday school as a child. He then agreed to leave. "This strengthens my belief that children should go to Sunday school. It gives them something for later in life," said Ms. Moffett. (*Toronto Star*)

John Youens, a sixty-three-year-old archdeacon and
chaplin to Queen Elizabeth II, was prosecuted in a British
court after detectives claimed that they saw Youens
repeatedly lift the skirt of a fourteen-year-old girl while
standing behind her at the Wimbledon tennis
championships. The veteran church figure escaped
conviction, however, when jurists chose to believe his
story that recent surgery made it necessary for him to
perform arm exercises that caused an accidental brush
with the teen-ager's garment. (*Chicago Tribune*)

It's bad enough being a loser in love, or to find yourself
last in the race, but for many losers, the ultimate disgrace
is to be without a job. Well, take heart you "also rans." To
have a job does not a winner make.

Vaudevillian Joseph Pujol performed at the Moulin Rouge in Paris by making use of his rear end. Blessed with an incredible talent for controlling his wind, Pujol would stand on stage and while bending over would perform a series of famous arias, using his escaping air. After blowing out a candle at a range of one foot the talented performer would complete his act by farting the Marseillaise as a solemn audience stood and sang along.

A waitress in an exclusive Dallas nightclub was given a million dollar tip by F. Masood Khon, a Pakistani businessman. After the party was over it was learned that Masood had contacted the First National Bank in Washington to stop payment on the check.

A London provincial newspaper reported Council workers are to rip planks out of seats and make holes in the walls of bus shelters in an attempt to make the shelters too uncomfortable for hooligans. Councillor Harry Bill said, "Something has got to be done to stop the wrecking of these shelters. So far as I can see, this is the only way."

Poland has entered the international high-fidelity-components market with a new record changer. Called the RSB-1, it has no tone arm and does not play records – it only changes them. "This is the first record changer that is doing exactly what its name indicates," said Wladislaw Woczorik, product engineer. "Our unit needs no tone arm to play records. You just plug it in – and it starts changing. It keeps on changing until you pull the plug. Besides," he added, "our changers produce a lot less noise than competing products." (*Audio Times*)

Strathclyde Regional Council's social work department has discovered 335 staff it did not know existed. (*Glasgow Herald*)

In 1978 Hans Mullikin, a thirty-nine-year-old Baptist minister from Marshall in Texas took on the job of paying President Carter a visit. He crawled 1,600 miles on his hands and knees to the gates of the White House only to be told that the President was too busy to see him.

Dorsey Evans, a lawyer from Detroit, recently accepted an offer to appear in a floor show at a Las Vegas nightclub. "I'm not a performer in the strict sense of the word," said Mr. Evans, "However, the management thought I would be of some interest to their customers because the two halves of the zipper in my trousers were welded together when I was struck by lightning. (*London Daily Mail*)

One hour after beginning a new job which involved moving a pile of bricks from the top of a two-storey house to the ground, a construction worker in Peterborough, Ontario, suffered an accident which hospitalized him. He was instructed by his employer to fill out an accident report. It read: "Thinking I could save time, I rigged a beam with a pulley at the top of the house, and a rope leading to the ground. I tied an empty barrel on one end of the rope, pulled it to the top of the house, and then fastened the other end of the rope to a tree. Going up to the top of the house, I filled the barrel with bricks. Then I went down and unfastened the rope to let the barrel down. Unfortunately, the barrel of bricks was now heavier than I, and before I knew what was happening, the barrel jerked me up in the air. I hung on to the rope, and halfway up I met the barrel coming down, receiving a severe blow on the left shoulder. I then continued on up to the top, banging my head on the beam and jamming my fingers in the pulley. When the barrel hit the ground, the bottom burst, spilling the bricks. As I was now heavier than the barrel, I started down at high speed. Halfway down, I met the empty barrel coming up, receiving several cuts and contusions from the sharp edges of the bricks. At this point, I must have become confused, because I let go of the rope. The barrel came down, striking me on the head, and I woke up in the hospital. I respectfully request sick leave." (*Toronto Star*)

111

A door-to-door magazine salesman had his solicitation permit revoked this week following numerous complaints concerning his sales methods. According to police, the offender, an employee of Opportunity Services Co. Inc., of Michigan City, Indiana, had called upon a local woman in the hopes of selling her a magazine subscription. When she failed to express sufficient interest, the salesman unzipped his trousers and urinated in her hallway. (*Iowa City Press Citizen*)

Young girl lavatory attendant wanted. Genial work. (*Bristol Mirror*)

A New York artist named Neke Carson paints portraits with his rear end. Carson inserts a paintbursh in his rectum, squats in a kneeling position, and puts his head between his legs. He recently used the technique, which he calls "Rectal Realism," to do a portrait of Andy Warhol. The drawing was executed with a pink felt-tip pen, which has a special rubberized shaft to facilitate penetration. Observers who saw the finished product described it as surprisingly realistic. "Boy, can that asshole paint," said one of Warhol's associates. (*Village Voice*)

Following the recent Supreme
Court decision returning the
power to define pornography to local
communities, the town of Clarkstown in
Rockland County, New York, recently established a nine
member "obscenity committee" to screen movies,
nightclub acts, and printed matter. It selected Harry
Snyder, a sixty-year-old retired restaurateur and business
man to head the committee.
Mr. Snyder is blind.
"My phone hasn't stopped ringing since," he remarked in
an interview at his home shortly after the appointment.
"We've attracted a lot of attention," he admitted. He
explained that other members of the obscenity committee
would sit next to him at screenings to "fill me in when the
screen goes silent." (*New York Times*)

Dick Edwards says that a strange substance has been falling from the sky and splattering his house. According to Edwards, his house is directly under a flight path, and he believes he's being hit by toilet debris as the johns are flushed just before landing. He reported the nuisance to the FAA and was told to watch for planes and note the registration number of any offending airliner. Refusing, Edwards said, "If they think I'm going to stand outside with my face to the sky, they're nuts." (*Moneysworth*)

The town of Walled Lake, Michigan, was having difficulty selling cemetery plots, and at the urging of mayor Bill Roberts, the city council decided to pass a resolution striking down a previous resolution which said that a person had to be dead to purchase a plot. "That could be part of the reason they're not selling too well," commented the mayor. (*Walled Lake Spinal Column*)

Sick of being surrounded by losers? Of course you are. Don't forget, the disease of loser is contagious. One touch of a loser's hand and it's off to the cellar in the standings. Escape. That's the answer. Get away from it all.

One hundred and three vacationers paid for a cruise billed as a "Trip to nowhere." They got exactly what they paid for. A few miles out of Norfolk, Virginia, the cruise ship *World Discovery* developed generator trouble and had to be hauled back to port.

An electricity supply account for $5 was returned by a consumer living in a select part of England. She told the electricity board that she was unable to pay because she had just returned from a world cruise on the QE2 and money was short. (*Eastbourne Herald*)

A half-million dollar lawsuit has been filed by a Texas widow who claims that the lack of sanitary toilet facilities aboard a seagoing vessel caused the death of her husband. Seaman Joseph J. Philson fell into the water and drowned last February 19, when, the lawsuit claims, "in response to a call of nature (he) was required to relieve himself by sitting on the railing of the vessel, which was the most sanitary method available since the toilet was not reasonably fit for its intended use and purpose." The owner of the ship, Saru, Inc., had also failed to provide suitable lifesaving equipment, and Philson could therefore not be rescued from his fall overboard.

Baines is an eccentric British millionaire who decided to take a cruise on the QE2 recently, but mistakenly thought he'd missed the departure from Southampton. So he chartered a jet to take him to Cherbourg, France, where he expected to catch the liner on its first stop. Only trouble was that when he got there he found the ship was still in Southampton, and he had to fly back. Cost of the charter flight: $6,000. (*Toronto Star*)

"Sirs, some years ago I was bringing a destroyer home from the Far East and was required to report my position twice a day. One evening I saw that we would be passing close to where the Greenwich Meridian touched the Equator, so I arranged to arrive there dead on midnight. Once there I altered my course so my position signal read:

At 00000 my position Latitude
00000 'N,' Longitude 00000 'E.'
Course 000. Speed 0.

I had considered saying I was nowhere but thought (probably correctly) that their Lordships would not be amused." (Letter To *The London Times*)

A German tourist Erwin Kreuz, en route from his native land to the West coast, stepped off his plane at a fueling stop in Bangor, Maine, and spent four days there thinking he was in California.

Mr. William Smith, a fifty-year-old lone sailor, set out
from Fraserburgh in Scotland to Great Yarmouth in
England in his seventy-five foot fishing vessel, *Excelsior*.
After missing the harbour at Bridlington by 400 yards
Smith ran aground.

Afloat once more, Smith crashed into a jetty where he
damaged the concrete docking.

A few hours later Mr. Smith went up on the beach at the
North foreland in Kent.

After being towed off he headed for Yarmouth unaware that Haven Bridge, which normally opens for shipping was closed by a strike. Mr. Smith was within 100 yards of the bridge before he realized that the bridge was not going to open. He turned away and was immediately caught by the tide. The *Excelsior* proceeded to crash into the ketch *Cereola* before hitting a dinghy.

Mr. Smith next struck the historic ship *Lydia*

before proceeding to crash into the *Scroly Queen*.

By now Smith had swung his boat clear, but in trying to move into an empty berth on the opposite bank Smith hit the coaster *Towaventure*.

From here he ran into the trimaran *Kala Kuma*.

At long last Mr. Smith slotted his boat in behind the *Gripen*, a 3,000-ton cargo ship. Unfortunately the ropes securing the *Gripen* to the quay became entangled in Mr. Smith's main mast.

Asked about the trail of damage in the harbour Mr. Smith said that you had to expect that kind of thing. "I don't know what all the fuss is about" said Smith before telling horrified reporters that he was now planning to sail to Australia.

For Some Losers There Is Only One Way Out...

Major Rowlandson, of Kenly, England, shot himself within a few minutes of the time when his insurance policy lapsed. The Westminster Coroner referred to the suicide as a "cold blooded method to defraud the company."

In Tallus, France, 1976, an unidentified seventy-seven-year-old man entered the medical department of a local University and made the following announcement; "Two years ago I agreed to donate my body to science and now I don't want to wait any longer. I have come here to finish myself off so that my body will be available immediately." He then drew a revolver from his pocket and blew out his brains. The trustees of the University accepted the body.

Sarah Ann Henlay jumped from the Clifton Suspension Bridge, Avon, England – a 250-foot fall. The year was 1885 and true to the dress of the day Sarah wore a long flowing garment complete with petticoat. Both billowed out and acted as a parachute bringing Sarah gently to earth unharmed.

Leo Klein of Port Elizabeth, South Africa, when attempting suicide found himself still alive after shooting himself through the head, slashing his wrists, hanging himself, and swallowing a jar of sleeping pills.

A murder-suicide pact between an eighty-nine-year-old man and his ninety-two-year-old wife failed because the weapon was almost as old as they were. Vancouver police reported that the man shot his wife in the head with an old .22-caliber pistol, but the rusty bullet ricocheted off a hair curler and the woman suffered only a scalp laceration. Then her husband's attempt to end it all met similar defeat when he put the gun to his right ear and fired. The shot was so weak that the bullet lodged in his right ear. The dazed man gave up and phoned a telephone operator who called the authorities. Police said the weapon had sat unused for at least sixty years. (*San Francisco Chronicle*)

After hearing that her husband was leaving her for another woman Mrs. Vera Czermak of Prague, Czechoslovakia flung herself from a third-storey window. Mrs. Czermak was taken to hospital, where she quickly recovered. Mr. Czermak, upon whom she landed, was killed instantly. (*Vecerny Pravda*).

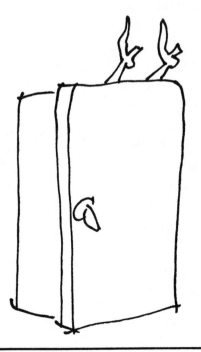

Fifty-two-year-old Eleanor Jones of Meeker, Colorado, decided to end her life when her husband walked out on her. She was a neat woman and was apparently concerned about being found decomposed, so she decided to freeze herself to death. She postponed her suicide for three days until she had eaten everything in the house. Then she crawled into her freezer and pulled the door shut. (*St. Louis Today*)

A twenty-seven-year-old electrician in Auckland, New Zealand, killed himself by rigging up an elaborate suicide machine that shot him six times in the heart while he was asleep. Police say the man whose name was not disclosed, lay down on a platform he had built which consisted of a series of snaplocks on chairs and wooden crossbars, designed so that if he changed his mind at the last minute, he could not escape. Electronic devices connected to two time clocks, one a backup in case the first failed, were set to fire a .22-caliber rifle through a hole in a board above the man's heart. If there had been a power failure, an electromagnet would have switched off, automatically pulling the trigger, and if anyone had entered the room, the opening of the door would have activated a mechanism which would have also fired the rifle.

After making the arrangements the man thoroughly cleaned the house, emptied and turned off the fridge, and left a note for the milkman telling him not to deliver any milk.

The man then took sleeping pills and locked himself in place on the platform. (*Milwaukee Journal*)

Charles V. Cunningham of Milwaukee was found by police after spending almost two days in an outhouse toilet. He was taken to Menomonee Falls Community Hospital suffering from exposure. The police said he was trying to commit suicide.

Workers in Menomonee County Park found Cunningham standing in about one foot of human waste in the woman's outhouse. His head was below the toilet seat. He was found after two children heard his cries for help. He was dressed only in some women's undergarments.
At first, Cunningham told police that someone had stuffed him down the toilet. Later he admitted he was trying to commit suicide. The police theorized that Cunningham thought he would drown in the contents of the toilet. But after he squeezed into the toilet through the hole, he couldn't get out, although he told police that he tried.
Police and park workers got him out of the toilet through a trap door in the rear usually used to clean out the contents. None could remember a suicide attempt like this. "If I were to commit suicide, I would have dived in," one officer said. (*Waukesha Daily Freeman*)

Many losers never made the book.
For this I am sincerely sorry.
Maybe next time.
Until then:

In the words of the barman seen talking to a particularly despondent customer in a *New Yorker* cartoon:

"So you're forty years of age. Look at it this way. If you were a horse you'd have already been dead twenty years."

Acknowledgements

For permission to reproduce excerpts from
Famous Flaws, by Alice Loomer, grateful
acknowledgement to Macmillan, Inc., New York.

For permission to reproduce excerpts from
Prima Donnas and Other Wild Beasts, by Alan
Wagner, grateful acknowledgement to Argonaut
Books, New Jersey.

Grateful acknowledgement is made to the following for
the photograph, page 19: Anthony Bruculere, *The Best of
Life* © 1973 Time Inc.

Without the actions of the many people mentioned in this
book it would have been impossible to produce. Not all
were losers. Among the winners are the newspapers that
first published the stories. My thanks to them and a
special thanks to the American publication *National
Lampoon* whose column "True Facts" first made me
aware of the fact that in being a loser, I am not alone.
George Gamester of the *Toronto Star* also gave valuable
help as did a number of people.

856789   659478   389587   349829   345829